HOW DOES IT WORK?

How Does a CAR Work?

BY SARAH EASON

Gareth Stevens
Publishing

Please visit our Web site www.garethstevens.com. For a free color catalog of all our high-quality books, call toll free 1-800-542-2595 or fax 1-877-542-2596.

Library of Congress Cataloging-in-Publication Data
Eason, Sarah.
    How does a car work? / Sarah Eason.
      p. cm. -- (How does it work?)
    Includes bibliographical references and index.
    ISBN 978-1-4339-3462-9 (library binding) -- ISBN 978-1-4339-3463-6 (pbk.)
    ISBN 978-1-4339-3464-3 (6-pack)
    1. Automobiles--Juvenile literature. 2. Mechanics--Juvenile literature. I. Title.
  TL147.E32 2010
  629.222--dc22   2009037154

Published in 2010 by
Gareth Stevens Publishing
111 East 14th Street, Suite 349
New York, NY 10003

© 2010 The Brown Reference Group Ltd.

For Gareth Stevens Publishing:
Art Direction: Haley Harasymiw
Editorial Direction: Kerri O'Donnell

For The Brown Reference Group Ltd:
Editorial Director: Lindsey Lowe
Managing Editor: Tim Harris
Editor: Sarah Eason
Children's Publisher: Anne O'Daly
Design Manager: David Poole
Designer: Paul Myerscough
Production Director: Alastair Gourlay

Picture Credits:
Front cover: Shutterstock: Mashe (background); Brown Reference Group (foreground)

Illustrations by Matthew White and Mark Walker

Picture Credits Key: t – top, b – below, c – center, l – left, r – right. Daimler Chrysler: 6; Ford Motor Company: 7t, 8, 10b, 13br, 14, 15tr, 20; Rover Group: 21t; Shutterstock: Konovalikov Andrey 25b, ArchMan 18, Oleg Babich 10, Victor Bernard 24, Mikael Damkier 5b, George Dolgikh 22, Domenic Gareri 26, Risteski Goce 9, Kklips 17b, Jonathan Larsen 28, PKM1 23, Michael Shake 29t, Stephen Sweet 12, Maksim Toome 7b, F Twitty 25t, Robert Young 27; TRW Aftermarket Operations: 17t; Wikipedia: 19b

Publisher's note to educators and parents: Our editors have carefully reviewed the Web sites that appear on p. 31 to ensure that they are suitable for students. Many Web sites change frequently, however, and we cannot guarantee that a site's future contents will continue to meet our high standards of quality and educational value. Be advised that students should be closely supervised whenever they access the Internet.

Printed in the United States of America
1 2 3 4 5 6 7 8 9   12 11 10

CPSIA compliance information: Batch #BRW0102GS: For further information contact Gareth Stevens, New York, New York at 1-800-542-2595.

Contents

How Does a Car Work?

The different parts of a car work together to make driving an easy, quick, and safe way of getting around. Modern cars are made up of around 14,000 parts.

The driver turns the car to the left and right using the steering wheel.

The engine burns gas to power the car.

The driver uses gears to change the speed of the car.

The suspension takes in bumps in the road to give a smooth ride.

The brakes bring the car to a controlled stop.

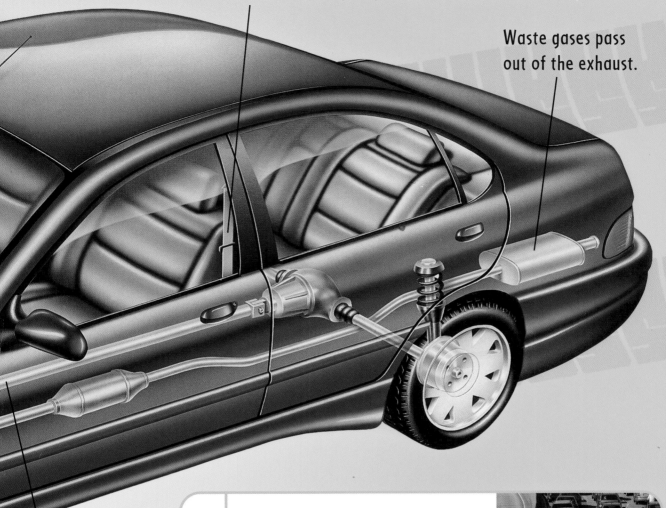

Seatbelts keep people in their seats if there is a crash. They help to prevent serious injuries.

Waste gases pass out of the exhaust.

The driveshaft transfers power from the engine to the wheels.

Fast Facts

- Every year, around ten million new cars are made in the United States.
- Every year, most drivers in the United States spend more than 18 days in their cars.

The First Cars

Modern cars are all based on an invention made in Germany more than 120 years ago.

Cars started out as steam-powered vehicles. A French scientist named Nicolas-Joseph Cugnot (1725–1804) invented the first one in 1769, but it didn't work very well. In 1803, English engineer Richard Trevithick (1771–1833) improved on the design, but the idea soon fell out of favor. People realized that steam carriages were dirty, heavy, and were also very inefficient.

Karl Benz drives his "Patent-Motor-Wagen"–one of the first cars with an internal combustion engine.

Internal combustion

In the late 1800s, two German engineers—Gottlieb Daimler (1834–1900) and Karl Benz (1844–1929)—came up with a new idea. They invented an internal combustion engine that used gasoline as a fuel. The new engines were small, light, and powerful. They were the ideal engines for cars.

The automobile industry

The first cars were expensive because they were made by

hand. Only the rich could afford them. In 1908, U.S. car maker Henry Ford (1863–1947) started to sell a new car, the Model T Ford. This car was made on a factory assembly line. Ford made millions of new Model Ts. Many people could then afford to buy a car.

Workers build a Model T Ford on a production line in 1914.

Modern cars

Modern cars come in many different shapes and sizes, but they all work on the same basic principle of the internal combustion engine.

THAT'S AMAZING!

The first automobile race took place in 1895. It was a 732-mile (1,178-kilometer) race from Paris to Bordeaux in France.

Modern cars are safe and efficient, and the designs are stylish.

The Engine

Most automobiles are powered by engines that burn a chemical called gasoline. The engine converts the energy released from burning the gasoline into the movement of the car.

The cylinders are the heart of an engine. This is where the gasoline and air mixture is set on fire by spark plugs. Most engines have four cylinders. Each cylinder is fitted with a piston. As each piston moves down the cylinder, it sucks gasoline and air through a valve. When the piston reaches the bottom of the cylinder, the valve closes.

This cutaway diagram shows the main parts of an engine that burns gasoline.

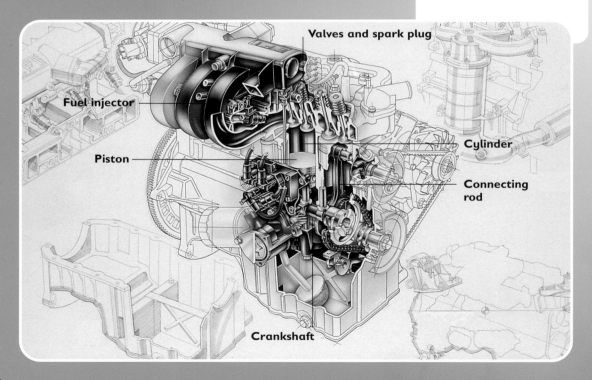

Valves and spark plug

Fuel injector

Piston

Cylinder

Connecting rod

Crankshaft

The engine fits under the hood of the car.

The piston moves back up the cylinder again. The movement squashes the gasoline and air in the cylinder. Just before the piston reaches the top of the cylinder, the spark plug creates a spark to set the fuel on fire.

No spark needed

Diesel engines work in a different way. The movement of the piston draws in air and squashes it until it becomes incredibly hot. A fuel called diesel is then forced into the cylinder. It burns very quickly in the hot air and drives the piston back down the cylinder.

The Four-stroke Cycle

1 The intake valve opens and the air and fuel enter the cylinder. The piston moves down.

Intake valve

Cylinder

Air/fuel mixture

Piston

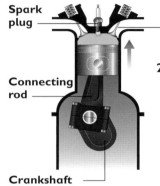

Spark plug

Exhaust valve

Connecting rod

Crankshaft

2 The intake valve and exhaust valve close. The piston moves up. This squashes the air and fuel mixture.

3 The spark plug creates a spark to set the air and fuel mixture on fire. The force from the explosion forces the piston back down the cylinder.

Ignition

Piston

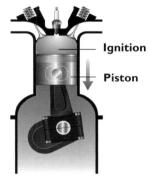

Exhaust valve

Burned gases

4 The piston moves up again. The exhaust valve opens to let out the burned gases. The whole process starts again.

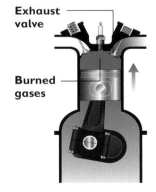

Waste Gases

The car's exhaust system changes harmful waste gases into less harmful substances that can be released into the air.

When fuel burns inside an engine, it produces waste gases. These include carbon dioxide, water vapor, and some poisonous gases. The waste gases must be removed so the engine can burn more fuel. The pistons force these gases out of the cylinders, through the exhaust pipe, and into the air.

Too much traffic on the highway pollutes the air.

Catalytic converter

A catalytic converter changes poisonous exhaust gases into less harmful waste products. The exhaust gases are forced through filters containing the metals platinum and rhodium. These metals speed up reactions between the gases. The gases are broken down to form other, less harmful gases, which are released from the exhaust pipe.

Gases are forced through the metal-coated filter

Filter containing metals

N_2 H_2O CO_2

Less harmful gases, such as nitrogen, water vapor, and carbon dioxide

NO_2 HC CO

Exhaust gases such as hydrocarbons, nitrogen oxide, and carbon monoxide

Clean and green

Poisonous gases pollute the air. Almost all modern cars are fitted with catalytic converters. They "convert" poisonous gases into less harmful products. The poisonous gases pass through a filter. Metals in the filter help to break them down. They form less harmful waste products, which do not cause as much damage to the environment. These waste products can then be released into the air.

Keeping quiet

The sound of the waste gases leaving the engine is very loud.

To deal with this problem, most modern cars are built with a device called a muffler, which is fitted to their exhaust system. A muffler greatly reduces the noise made by the waste gases by releasing them gradually instead of all at once.

Gearing Up

Gears allow cars to drive at different speeds and tackle different road conditions. Low gears help drivers pull away or drive up steep hills. High gears help drivers gain speed once the car is moving.

In first gear, the engine turns very quickly, but the drive wheels move much more slowly. The driver uses first gear to pull away from a standing start or drive up very steep hills. The driver uses second gear to drive up steep hills and increase the speed if the car is already moving. Third and fourth gears

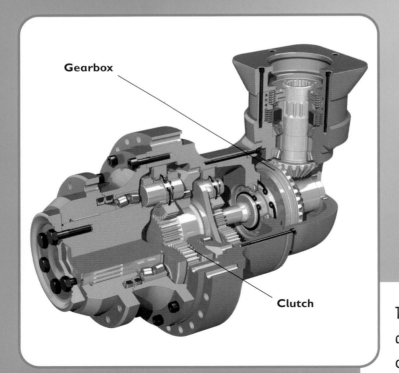

Gearbox

Clutch

THAT'S AMAZING!

Some cars have an automatic gearbox, which changes gears without the driver pressing a clutch pedal.

This cutaway diagram shows a clutch and gearbox.

Make your own gears

You can make a system that shows exactly how the gears in a car's gearbox work.

You will need:
• poster board • scissors • thumbtacks
• thick cardboard

1 Trace the shapes of these gear wheels onto the poster board. Cut them out.

2 Pin the gear wheels onto the thick cardboard backing. Arrange them in a line, from the smallest to the largest. Mark a dot at the top of each gear wheel.

3 Now count how many times the smaller gear wheels must turn for just one turn of the largest gear wheel.

are used as the car gains more speed. These gears are much larger, and the drive wheels turn much faster as a result.

Changing gear

In most cars, drivers change gears by using a gearstick and a clutch pedal. The clutch pedal separates the engine from the transmission (the system that transfers power from the engine to the wheels). The driver can then move the gearstick to select a new gear.

Gears

This diagram shows how the gearstick attaches to the gearbox. The driver presses a clutch pedal with his or her foot to engage the clutch. The driver then moves the gearstick to change between gears.

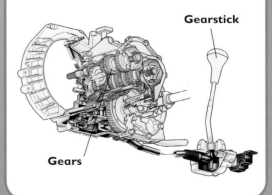

Gearstick

Gears

Suspension and Steering

A car's suspension system absorbs bumps in the road to give a smooth ride. The steering system allows the driver to turn the car in the right direction.

The suspension system smooths out the ride using strong, thick springs. There are four springs in total—one for each wheel. Shock absorbers stop the car from bouncing around on the springs. The shocks gradually remove the energy in the springs to smooth out the ride.

This picture shows the arrangement of suspension system and shock absorbers on a Ford automobile.

Steering system

The driver turns a steering wheel to turn the car. The steering wheel connects to a gear system, which transfers the movement of the steering wheel into the movement of the wheels. When a car takes a corner, the wheel on the outside of the bend travels farther than the wheel on the inside. A system of gears called the differential allows each wheel to turn at different speeds round the corner.

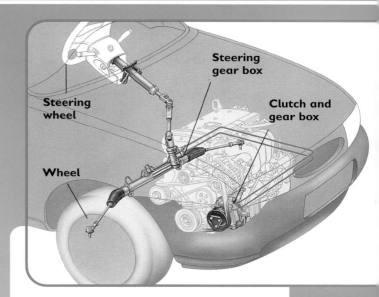

Steering gear box

Steering wheel

Clutch and gear box

Wheel

This diagram shows the power steering assembly that makes it easier to turn the wheels of a car.

Differential

The differential allows the front wheels to turn at different speeds as the car takes a corner.

Larger cog powers the wheels

Smaller cogs allow the wheels to rotate separately

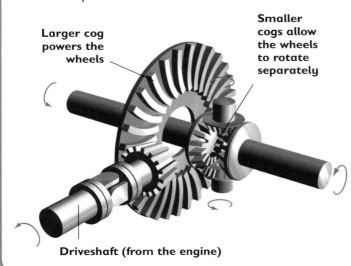

Driveshaft (from the engine)

THAT'S AMAZING!

Tires on the wheels of a car are filled with air. This is another part of the car's suspension system. The tires smooth out the ride on rough roads.

Braking System

The brakes are one of the most important parts of a car. Without them, the driver cannot stop.

Brakes transfer the pushing force on a brake pedal at the driver's feet to slow the car. When the driver pushes on the pedal, the force of his or her foot pushes down on an oily liquid, called brake fluid, inside a tube. The tube connects the brake pedal to the brake pad. The brake fluid transfers the pushing force to the brake pad. The brake pad then clamps on the brake disk to slow the car. Transmitting forces through liquids is known as hydraulics.

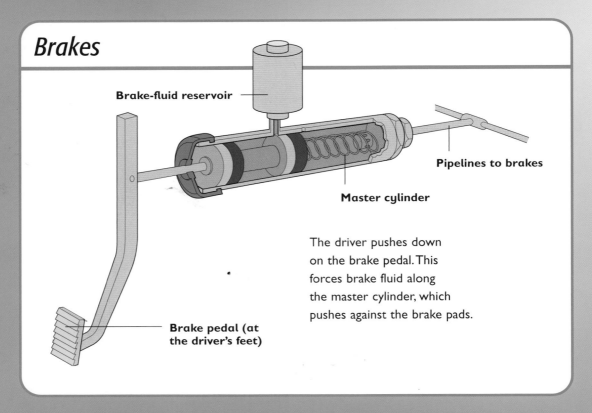

Brakes

Brake-fluid reservoir

Pipelines to brakes

Master cylinder

The driver pushes down on the brake pedal. This forces brake fluid along the master cylinder, which pushes against the brake pads.

Brake pedal (at the driver's feet)

Tire wall

Hydraulic
fluid inlet

Brake
housing

Brake pad

Revolving
disk

A cutaway diagram shows the brake system. The brake pads clamp down on the brake disk, which revolves on the wheel. Gradually, the car slows down.

Brake power

In most cars, the brake system steals power from the engine to increase the pushing force of the driver's foot. By doing this, the brake pads will clamp down on the brake disk much harder. That makes the car slow much more quickly.

Other ways to slow a car

If brakes fail, the best way to slow is to change down through the gears. First, take the foot off the gas—the engine slows with less fuel to burn. Aerodynamics and friction then slow the car. The handbrake can be used in an emergency to stop the car.

THAT'S AMAZING!

Dragsters move so quickly that brakes alone could not stop them. Parachutes work alongside the brakes to help slow down the car.

Wheels

A car rolls along the road on four wheels. The wheels need to be strong to both support the weight of the car and absorb any bumps in the road.

The wheels are important because they are the car's contact point with the road. They bolt onto axles, which connect the wheels to the driveshaft. Most wheels are made of steel, but many sports cars have alloy wheels. These lightweight wheels improve handling and make the car go faster.

The tires

The first cars had metal wheels with wooden rims, and the ride was very bumpy. Modern cars have air-filled tires to smooth out the ride. The tires are made from thick rubber, which stops the tire from shredding as it moves along the road. The grooves in the tire, called the tread, help the tire grip the road.

Groove

The tires of sports cars have deep grooves to help grip the road as the car moves.

Try the friction slide test

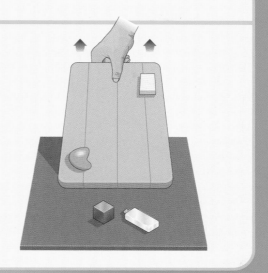

1 Collect a range of different materials: glass, stone, metal, rubber, and wood. Then put the different materials on the edge of a wooden board. Lift up the board and watch the materials slide all the way down the board.

2 Some materials grip the board better than others. This gripping force is called friction. Tires need to grip the road so they do not slide—that's why they are made from rubber.

Tire change

Race car tires are made from a special rubber that grips the road tightly but wears out quickly. Race cars must stop to have their tires changed at least once during a race. A team of mechanics wait in the pit lane ready for the car to pull in. There are usually two mechanics on each wheel. One unscrews and tightens the bolts. The other changes the wheel. They do this within seconds.

Fast Facts

- *Scottish scientist Robert William Thomson (1822–1873) invented the first air-filled tires in 1846.*
- *Another Scottish scientist, John Boyd Dunlop (1840–1921; right), made the tire a commercial success.*

Bodywork

The bodywork is the outer shell of a car. It protects all the different parts inside the car and gives the car a streamlined shape.

Car makers design cars to cut through the air with minimum drag. Streamlined, or aerodynamic, designs make cars faster and more stable, and they use less fuel.

Size and shape

Different cars are used for different purposes. Vans are used to carry heavy loads from place to place. This is why most vans

Engineers test the aerodynamics of a Ford automobile. The white lines are streams of air passing over the car.

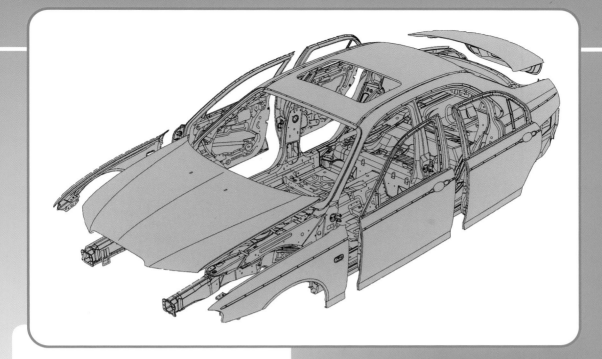

The body panels are welded onto the main chassis. This gives the car extra strength.

have boxlike shapes—it gives them a lot of storage space. Sports cars have powerful engines and move quickly. They have streamlined bodywork.

Modern materials

Heavy steel panels were once used to make bodywork. Car makers now use aluminum, lighter metal alloys, and high-tech materials such as carbon fiber. These are strong and light. A lighter car is more efficient because it burns less fuel.

TRY FOR YOURSELF

Shape up

Try this activity if you are sitting in a car on a long journey. Look at some of the shapes of cars on the road. Sketch them with a pencil. Older cars are not very aerodynamic—they look like boxes on wheels. Modern cars are sleek and streamlined. Older cars do not move as quickly as modern cars, and therefore aerodynamics is not as important.

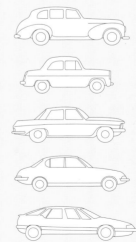

At the Controls

Modern cars are designed with driver and passenger comfort in mind.

Car makers put a lot of thought into the design of the interior, from the floor right up to the roof. For example, carpets on the floor make the interior look stylish. But they also make car journeys quieter by absorbing some of the noise from the engine.

Fun Facts

In-car navigation systems help drivers get to their destination. The driver inputs the destination, and the computer provides the directions.

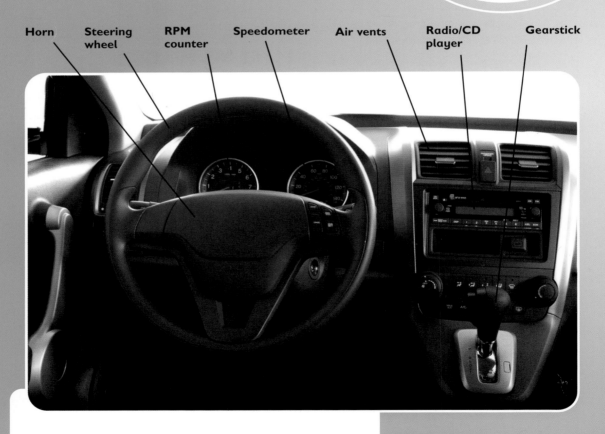

Horn Steering wheel RPM counter Speedometer Air vents Radio/CD player Gearstick

The dashboard contains all the control devices of the car.

THAT'S AMAZING!

Many modern cars now come fitted with satellite navigation as standard. These devices use global positioning system (GPS) satellites to fix the position of the car on a road map. The position is displayed on a monitor in the middle of the dashboard.

Car seats can be adjusted to fit people of different sizes. They support the back and neck to make long trips comfortable. The seats at the front slide forward and backward so the driver can reach the pedals while giving the passengers behind enough leg room.

In the driver's seat

Controls are positioned within reach so the driver does not have to take his or her hands off the wheel. Dials such as the speedometer and fuel gauge are positioned so the driver can see them without needing to take his or her eyes off the road.

Fast Facts

- *Luxury cars usually come fitted with leather seats. Most ordinary cars have seats made from plastic and cheaper fabric.*
- *By law, babies and children have to sit in special car seats to keep them safe and comfortable when the car is moving.*

Safety First

Every year, there are millions of car accidents in the United States. Sometimes people die. Safety measures such as fitting airbags, seatbelts, and solid construction make driving much safer than before.

Airbags and seatbelts stop a lot of serious injuries. During a crash, airbags pop out of the steering wheel and dashboard and fill with air. They absorb the impact of the driver and front passenger as they are thrown

Airbags inflate during a crash to protect the driver and front seat passenger.

Improved safety measures mean that most car crashes do not cause serious injuries.

Car manufacturers learn how to make cars safer by using crash test dummies in car crashes. The crash test dummies move like people would in a real crash. Car makers look at how the dummies move in a crash and see where they need to improve passenger safety.

forward. Seatbelts lock tight to stop people from being thrown forward during a crash.

Crumple zones

Car makers design cars with "crumple zones" that collapse during a crash. These are usually at the front and rear of the car. They absorb the force of a crash, to keep people in the car safe.

Antilock brakes

Drivers usually slam on the brakes to avoid crashes. This makes the brakes lock up, the car skids, and the driver loses control. Modern cars are fitted with antilock braking systems (ABS). ABS allows the driver to brake hard and steer out of danger without skidding.

On the Race Track

People have been racing cars for almost as long as cars have been around. There are many different races today, from Formula One and IndyCar to rally cars and hot rods.

The first car race took place in 1895 between Bordeaux and Paris in France. The winner traveled an average of 15 miles (25 kilometers) per hour. Modern race cars can accelerate to more than 200 miles (320 kilometers) per hour.

Formula One

Formula One races have been held since World War I (1914–1918). Over the decades, car makers have come up with new ideas to make Formula One cars faster and easier to drive. ABS, traction control, and improved aerodynamics were all developed for Formula One but are now common in normal cars.

Formula One is the most popular motorsport in Europe.

IndyCar

IndyCar racing is the U.S. version of Formula One. The most famous track is the Indianapolis Motor Speedway.

Drag cars are timed along a track called the drag strip. The fastest car wins the race.

Other race cars

Hot rods are popular in the United States. Hot rods are normal cars that are modified for racing. Rally car racing is popular in Europe. Cars race on normal roads and special trails. The driver follows a set route, guided by a navigator in the car.

Cars of the Future

Cars of the future will need to run on different fuels. The world's supply of gasoline is running out. Burning gasoline produces harmful gases that are polluting the planet.

Alternative fuel vehicles are cars that run on fuels other than gasoline or diesel. Biofuels are already a popular alternative to gas-powered cars. Other ideas also include electric cars that are powered by batteries and fuel cells.

An electric car plugs into a power socket to charge up the batteries.

Biofuels

Many modern cars run on fuels made from plants, called biofuels. The fuel comes from the oils in plant seeds or by turning sugars in the plants into alcohol. The alcohol is used as the fuel. Biofuels are good because they work in normal gasoline and diesel engines. The problem is that growing the plants takes up space needed to grow food crops. Biofuels also produce some pollution.

Electric cars

Most electric cars run on electricity stored in rechargable batteries. An electric motor powers the car. These cars are good for the environment because they produce no pollution. They are also quiet and efficient.

- Solar-powered cars generate their own electricity using the energy from sunlight.
- Hybrid cars (right) run on a combination of gasoline and electricity.

The problem with these cars is their batteries. They cannot store a lot of electricity so electric cars cannot travel long distances.

Hydrogen cars

Scientists think that fuel cells are the answer to the problem. Fuel cells are like batteries. Fuel cells convert hydrogen gas and oxygen from the air into water. The cell generates electricity at the same time. Cars with fuel cells are quiet and run over much longer distances than electric cars. The fuel cells themselves are very clean, but making the hydrogen these cars need as fuel does pollute the environment.

Glossary

accelerate: to move faster

acidic: a very strong substance that can eat away at materials, including metals

aerodynamics: the way air moves over things. The more streamlined an object is, the more easily air will pass over it.

airbag: inflatable plastic bag that blows up to create a soft cushion in the event of a crash. The cushion protects the passenger or driver.

aluminum: a type of metal

biofuel: a fuel made from rapeseed

bodywork: the metal covering of a car. The bodywork surrounds the car's frame and engine.

brakes: part of a car that forces it to stop. The brakes are controlled by the driver.

catalytic converter: part of the car that converts harmful gases into less harmful ones

clutch pedal: pad near the driver's feet which, if pressed, allows the driver to use the brake or gears without stalling the car

cylinders: parts of a car in which gas and air are mixed to create energy to power the car forward

dashboard: part of the car in front of the driver's seat. The dashboard contains many of the driver's controls.

dragster: a type of racing car

engine: part of a car that powers it forward

engineer: person who can design, construct, or maintain a machine such as a car

exhaust: tube at the back of the car through which waste gases are released into the air

friction: a force that stops something, such as a car, from moving

fuel guage: device on a car's dashboard that shows how much fuel is in the gas tank

gas: collection of atoms. Gas is used in cars to create an energy that drives the car forward.

gasoline: a fuel used to create an energy that powers a car forward

gear: part of a car that helps to control the speed at which the car travels

gearbox: part of the engine that holds the gears

gearstick: a stick next to the driver that he or she can use to change gear

internal combustion: the conversion of gases into a fuel or energy that can power a car

muffler: part of the car that reduces the sound heard outside the car when the engine is switched on

pollute: to pass harmful gases into the atmosphere

seatbelt: a belt that holds the passenger or driver safely in their seat

spark plugs: part of the car that ignites or sets fire to fuel to create an energy that powers the car forward

speedometer: device on the car's dashboard that shows the speed at which it travels

steering wheel: wheel positioned in front of the driver's seat and used to steer the car

suspension: system within a car that reduces the impact felt by the passenger and driver as the car drives over a bump in the road

trails: race tracks that are off normal roads. Trails might be in woods or in fields.

valve: a small part of the car that controls the flow of fuel in the engine

Further Information

Books to read:

Graham, Ian. *Fast Cars: How They Work.* New York, NY: Franklin Watts, 2008.

Hammond, Richard. *Car Science.* New York, NY: Dorling Kindersley, 2008.

Web sites to look at:

www.japanauto.com

www.hfmgv.org

Museums to visit:

Motor Sports Hall of Fame, Novi, MI.
www.mshf.com

Museum of Automobile History, Syracuse, NY.
http://www.themuseumofauto mobilehistory.com

Index